For athletes everywhere.

Remember, you are not alone in this.

Introduction:

I decided to write this book after some serious encouragement from my dear friend, ESPN Basketball Analyst Sean Farnham. I told him about a project I was involved with and later that day received a call from him in shock saying, "If you don't turn this into a book by next summer, consider that a failure." Over a year later and well past that summer, I finally found the courage to do it.

Here is why...

Sports psychologists from The University of Southern California approached me in

2010 about doing an on camera interview for the exiting seniors. They told me the video was to cover issues that transitioning athletes had dealt with upon "retirement," whether it was due to injury, illness or graduation. The department felt the majority of student athletes were not well prepared at the close of their careers and were unsure of what to expect. This was supposed to open up the lines of communication and bring honesty and frankness to such a mysterious, misunderstood subject.

I decided to do the interview. I was extremely passionate about this already and felt like my alma mater was taking steps in the right direction to help prepare their athletes for life after sports. What I didn't realize is how upset and emotional I still was about my own retirement from my beloved sport of volleyball, even two years later. Needless to say, the interview opened up Pandora's box of tears.

At the time, I was writing a weekly blog for Fox Sports West on USC sports. My blog covered the teams of the spring season, the wins, losses, and everything in between. The week following my interview, I decided I would be temporarily taking my blog in a new direction. And no, I did not ask permission. This is what I submitted,

which was published on the site that
following Monday.

"No One Ever Tells You What To Do When
It's Over

By Kelli Tennant

I got a call this week from the athletic
department at USC. They asked me if I
would be willing to come in and be
interviewed along with some other former
athletes for a video segment they are
producing for next year.

The video will be presented to the
graduating seniors at the end of each year

as a way to open up the lines of communication about life after sports. It will cover topics including schedule changes, losing motivation to be active, finding a new passion, etc.

I was thrilled to hear this, and of course said "yes." My first thought was, "It's about time!"

In 2008, I was forced to retire from volleyball due to an autoimmune disease. The transition for me from devout athlete to "normal person" was probably the most difficult time in my life... outside of dealing with the actual symptoms of the disease.

At first, I went crazy. I had so much free time on my hands, I decided I would make up for all the years I missed out on parties and other social activities. So I headed out, almost every night and became the social butterfly. It was a way to not deal with what I was going through on the inside, and I put on a façade as if I was actually excited to not have volleyball in my life anymore.

Then came the eating disorder. That was definitely a low point for me. I had my family and friends relentlessly commenting on how skinny I was getting and my mom would always bring up how "weird" I looked. I later realized she referring to my sunken in face and ribs sticking out. I kept covering up the fact that I was not eating by constantly saying how full I was, or how much I had eaten at the previous meal. I dropped about 20 pounds in four months and was incredibly weak and hungry all the time.

I was on a very heavy dose of several medications, from painkillers, to anti-depressants to muscle relaxers. This was definitely a concern because not only did they make me feel like I was going crazy, but the chances of an overdose were pretty high, accidental or not.

One of my teammates showed up at my apartment one morning, screaming and banging on the door. I opened it up and she was crying and jumped at me and hugged me. I had no clue what was going on. She told me that my mom and boyfriend had been trying to get a hold of me all morning and when I did not answer my phone for a few hours, they imagined the worst. I was clearly "ok", but when I realized how worried everyone was about me all the time, for my health and life, it was truly eye opening. Apparently I was not hiding my feelings from everyone as well as I thought.

It wasn't until my meeting with the USC Nutritionist (forced by my mom) that I realized exactly what I was doing to myself, and why it was happening. I sat down with Kristy Morrell and she immediately started quizzing me about my eating habits, my calorie obsessing, my daily routines, and feelings about the loss of volleyball and how I was handling it all. The truth finally came out: **I had lost control over everything in my life** and food was the last thing I could keep a solid grasp of. At that moment, I became conscious of how much of a downward spiral I was in.

Right around the time I had my eating habits back under control and had stopped going out so much, I found a new doctor. Long story short, he took me off all of the medications I was on, put me on something without any side effects and made some huge improvements. But I was still left with a lot of time needing to be filled.

I spent my time in rehabilitation, physical therapy, working out, classes and broadcasting. I began seeing significant changes in my physical strength and endurance and my mood was becoming lighter and brighter and things started looking up.

I had always wanted to get into broadcasting, and when I approached the athletic department about this, my coaches, the video department and sports information directors didn't hesitate to help. I had been doing things here and there with internships, but this was the moment when things took off and I immersed myself in reporting. I had found my passion, a new career and something to put my time and energy into. It literally saved me.

I look back and think about how rough those couple years were. I am thankful to now feel significantly better and in control of most things in my life. But it is scary to think about what would have happened had I not found something to turn to after sports. As athletes, we spend our entire lives preparing to compete and win at the highest level. But **no one ever tells you what to do when it is over**. And it is always over for everyone, at some point or another.

Life changes dramatically and that's the honest truth. Maybe we try to protect athletes from the reality of life, or maybe we just believe they will figure it out on their own. But why? We have classes for students about getting jobs, there are opportunities for career counseling, but there is never a class on what to do when your coach is not scheduling your life for you, or how to eat when you are not training six hours a day or how to deal with the loss of a life-long love.

I am so thrilled that USC is taking the initiative to create this type of presentation for the athletes. I know there is more that can and should be done, but this is an amazing way to start. We have to be willing to be open about the harsh realities sometimes; otherwise we are just doing them a disservice and possibly setting them up for short and potentially long term struggles."

Following the post of this blog, I received an incredible number of responses through emails, Facebook messages and phone calls. Most people were shocked I had gone through any of this. I call myself the best liar in town because I know how to fake a smile better than anyone, even when my leg felt as though it was going to fall off and I did not want to live anymore. Other people were extremely touched by my honesty. And others were relieved. I cannot tell you how many former athletes from different universities came forward and said, "Thank you for writing this. I thought I was the only person going through this." That is when I knew that although unintentional, I had started down a road less traveled.

I want the words on these pages to serve as a guide for athletes, coaches, parents and administrators everywhere. I want you to hear it from the people who've gone through it, to understand we are all in this together. The cheering will stop. This book is to help prepare you before that day comes so you have the tools to make the transition, successfully.

In these pages you will find not only my personal story which is always evolving, along with those of my friends, my mentors, others I respect and even stories from anonymous contributors who wanted their stories to be heard. When read in their entirety, these narratives will aid in your transitional journey. These stories will address the physical impact and the mental and emotional struggle, as well as how to handle the various challenges you face as you learn to accept a new identity, and lastly, a collaborative, unique game plan designed to fit specific needs and preferences. It is my hope after reflecting on these stories and actively applying key concepts from this handbook that you feel relieved that what you are feeling is normal while having a sense of confidence in your abilities and in your optimism about the future.

As you reflect and apply the messages contained herein, you may begin to wonder why it is so "Southern California heavy." It is simply because this is my lived experience and I feel comfortable sharing my life with you. My friends, colleagues, mentors and anonymous contributors share this same notion. By including stories from others along with my own, it was a way to galvanize the experiences of many, regardless of who you are and where you are from. I am aware things are different from state to state, school to school, know that regardless of these different variables, the feelings can be the same. Despite me being a Trojan through and through, I am first and foremost a former athlete who hopes to help you along your transitional adventure.

I am also aware many of you may not be ready to read every chapter, just yet. Do so at your own pace and don't be afraid to reference it again later on as issues or questions arise. Below is a description of what The Transition means, as this book focuses on better understanding and improved awareness and acceptance of its challenges as you navigate its unforgiving terrain.

The Transition:

In Schlossberg's Transition Theory, a transition is "any event or non event that results in changed relationships, routines, assumptions, and roles." 1 Transitions are all about perception. The three transition types are anticipated, unanticipated or a nonevent. Transitions have context and are determined by the individuals relationship to the environmental setting in which the transition is occurring. For example, in my case, I had a rather tumultuous experience because of the pain and the fact that it was not my choice to end my career, but also a very supportive group of people around me.

There are four factors which affect one's
ability to cope with transition and they
include: situation, self, support, and
strategies.

- Situation: Trigger (what ignites
  an emotion or feeling), timing
  (when it happens in your life),
  control (whether or your terms
  or forced due to injury, illness
  or retirement), role change
  (from athlete to a new
  identity), duration (how long it
  lasts until you are fully
  transitioned), previous
  experience with a similar
  transition (going to college
  from high school or

retirement from another activity), concurrent stress (other factors creating a sense of uneasiness), assessment (analyzing the current situation).

- Self: Two kinds: personal and demographic characteristics (gender, age, health, ethnicity, culture, etc.) and cultural resources (ego development, outlook, commitment, resilience, spirituality, self-efficacy, values, etc.)
- Support: Types (intimate, family, friends, institutional), functions (affects,

affirmations, aid, honest feedback) and measurements (stable and changing supports).

- Strategies: These include three categories– Modify the situation (change the current status, control the meaning of the problem (decide what meaning you allow the issue to have over you), or aid in the managing of stress afterwards (walking yourself through the pain or suffering caused by transition, understanding its effects and dealing with them rationally and fairly).

- Four coping models: information seeking (finding out why this has happened or what can be learned from it), direct action (being proactive about how to handle the situation and not avoiding it), inhibition of action (limiting yourself from handling the situation, denying the reality or putting it off), intrapsychic behavior. 2

In Chapter 1, we dive into the

identity shift from athlete to a

revised version of you.

Chapter 1

Identity Crisis: defining the new version of you

"It's the deepest, darkest, quietest place you've ever been. You don't know which direction to go. I've played baseball my whole life, and I know I can do that well. I can compete with anyone at anything physically. But when your body goes, what do you do then? You have to totally reinvent yourself. There's some self-doubt there. You have to go find the confidence." Mike Hampton, Major League Baseball

This is the greatest obstacle most athletes face. Losing your identity as an athlete and not knowing whom you are anymore is the root of every problem that will be discussed in this book.

Most team sport athletes spend their entire youth playing sports. It may not be just one specific sport, yet they immerse themselves in a competitive, team atmosphere for years. This creates a sense that "sports are everything" which in turn leads to "sports are my life." Although playing a sport is positive for many reasons, this kind of mindset can lead to the pain and anguish some experience upon retirement.

When all we know is sports and we haven't found another outlet to place our passion, we may lose ourselves. In this way, we no longer play the sport, the sport plays us.

When we are defined as "athlete," we are labeled as so because of the way we look, dress, workout, eat, sleep, manage time, and socialize. When every single one of these aspects of who we are changes, we no longer have that identity. So we begin to search for our new label. But the problem most of us can run into is we have not spent much time figuring out what else it is we enjoy doing or want to spend our lives pursuing. So we are stuck in a proverbial rut trying to decide who this new person is.

A few years back, a good friend and fellow student athlete at SC almost had her last hoorah, or so we thought. Jacki Gemelos, a stud basketball player, tore her ACL for the fifth time as a sixth year senior. Now, I'm sure most people read that line multiple times because it's a shocking number. What's even more shocking is that against all odds, this woman has played in the WNBA and was the 26th overall pick in the 2012 Draft.

Jacki was a year younger than me in college. We created a friendship over the years and after I had to retire, I watched her own journey. One after the next, the girl could not catch a break. Every time, we would have a chat about it on campus or on the platforms of the weight room, and it was always the same question: "Are you going to come back?" I hesitated asking because I knew the feeling she was having to some extent. Jacki always asked what I thought she should do. I tried to help her weigh the pros and cons while being honest with her. But ultimately there's no right choice in this situation, and it's her life, not mine.

She simply came back every year. Just like Brett Favre, some people would call her crazy. But I was not one of them. Jacki is the epitome of not knowing what to do after it is over. She had the dream prep career– #1 recruit, Miss CA Basketball, McDonald's All-American. She was hard working, talented, and a team player with a bright future. And Jacki, even with a completely dysfunctional lower body, multiple surgeries and emotional agony, couldn't let go of the hope that she would see her dreams through on the court.

Off the court, she had so much going for her– an undergraduate degree and masters from USC, in addition to her intelligence, drive, work ethic, leadership, and inner beauty. The employer's dream!

Then of course there was the alumni network and her personal network of wonderful family and friends.

But to Jacki, that was not enough. She, in her mind, was not enough without basketball as her true identity. Jacki wanted to wake up, go to shoot around, lift and play. And I get it. How many years had she spent in this routine? It was all she knew and what she believed to be normal. Anything less would be just, weird.

I am so empathetic to what she's gone through and I'm sure you are as well. It's every athlete's biggest nightmare, and she has had to deal with it for years. The fear of not playing is more painful than the actual pain of injuries and the emotional rollercoaster.

When you feel like a washed up athlete that used to once shine brightly under the lights and hear the roars of a crowd screaming your name, the chances of you losing your mind are highly probable.

So how do you combat this? Well there are a number of ways. The first is to cope with the fact that you are not, and never were, just an "athlete." You are a human, a person with emotions, talents and things to offer outside of your sport. Maybe you already know this from being involved in different activities or clubs, or maybe you have no idea because you have dedicated your life to your sport and never ventured outside those lines.

My dear friend and host of ESPN's SportsNation, Marcellus Wiley, shed some light on identity when we talked about this. At seven years old, his grandmother sat him down and had him write down his name and three things he believed he was. When he completed that, she said, "Okay, good. Any time someone calls you one of these things, answer them. If they call you anything else, don't answer." This is a rule he has lived by since that day. And because of that, he always knew, football or not, he was and is athletic, smart and nice. He said to me, "It's never too late to identify who you are. You can always add or evolve."

If you are like Marcellus and already know you are more than just your sport, do your best to rediscover the things you love. Ask yourself:

Who am I?

What matters most to me?

Where do I want to go from here?

What impact have I had on others outside of my sport?

How am I going to impact the world?

Where can my other interests fit in to create a new life for myself?

Then commit yourself to the answers to those questions. The Transition is not easy, but the sooner you find those passions and spend your energy with them, the sooner you realize there was always more to you than your identity as the "athlete."

If you are someone who never saw life outside of your sport, things will be a bit more difficult, but still manageable. I find that most people are prone to this second mindset, as most parents have fostered this type of environment. Many children focus on their Little League, then travel ball, then high school, then college. All the while with hopes of "making it."

Let us look at what the statistics have to say. According to the NCAA statistics on the odds of playing college sports, 3.1% of high school boys basketball players end up on a college team. In football, 6%, baseball, 6.4%, women's basketball, 3.5%.

According to an article in The Sport Digest, in men's basketball there is only a .03% chance of playing professionally. Of the 156,000 male high school senior basketball players, only 44 will be drafted to the NBA. In football, the odds are slightly better as .08% or 250 of 317,000 high school seniors will be drafted. 3

Even with these odds, there is rarely a talk of, "if I don't make it, what will I do?" So because this question is not asked and because most gifts this child has ever gotten have been baseball related, why would he ever feel the urge to find something else? He wouldn't and doesn't. He must now start from scratch. Although unconscious in most cases, this person clearly identifies himself solely with being a baseball player. When asked what his story is, rarely will he start with: "I'm a smart, giving, loving person that enjoys activities such as baseball." Rather, he will say he's "a baseball player and wants to play in the pros someday." Yes, kids should have amazing dreams. But do you see how this will deeply affect him when he's done? All the value he places on himself and his life lies in baseball. So when the sport is gone, the value is gone.

To help redefine this mindset, I find a great way to figure out your passion is to brainstorm and write things down. Write down everything that comes to mind. Any profession that sounds exciting and anything that brings you joy. For example, you can use things you learned about yourself during athletics to help this process. As an athlete, you probably traveled a lot, spent time working out, were interviewed by media, held a strict routine that was the same every day but never in the same place, and flourished in the competitive atmosphere. What can you do that brings all those things out? Or maybe you traveled extensively and actually hated that aspect of it, so you know you will not want to travel.

So I ask, what do you want to be remembered for?
What do you want people to say about you?
What do you want to be able to say about yourself?
What regrets do you not want to have?

Once you find the answers to those questions, your path to a more adaptive transition will become clearer.

I sat down with my former classmate at USC, Rebecca Soni. Just eight months removed from her second Olympics, she was considering retirement. Rebecca's swimming accomplishments are remarkable. She won the Gold Medal and set a World Record in the 200m breaststroke at the Beijing Olympic Games. Rebecca also took home 2 Silver Medals in the 100m breaststroke and the 4x100m medley relay. In the spring, she ended her collegiate career at USC by sweeping both breaststroke events at NCAA

Championships. Her win in the 200y was

done in American Record time and she

broke the NCAA record in the 100y. Her

career at USC was flawless – she was a 6–

time NCAA Champion, winning in the 200y

breaststroke all 4 years. In London,

Rebecca won her first medal, a silver, in

the 100m breaststroke. Two days later,

after breaking the world record in the

semifinals with a time of 2:20.00, Rebecca

won a gold medal in the final of the 200m

breaststroke with a time of 2:19.59,

breaking her own world record and

becoming the first woman ever to break 2

minutes 20 seconds in the event. With her

win, Rebecca became the first female to

successfully defend her title in the event.
In her final event, the 4x100m medley
relay, she won gold with Missy Franklin,
Dana Vollmer and Allison Schmitt.
Swimming the breaststroke leg, she
recorded a time of 1:04.82, and the U.S.
team went on to set a new world record
with a time of 3:52.05.

After Beijing, she began to think about the
future. She asked herself, "What do I
want?" She was constantly reminded in
every media interview, just seconds out of
the pool, "Will you be back in four years?"
She started wondering what the point of it
all was and whether or not it mattered if
she was there or not.

After some time away, she decided to get back into training and give it another try. As you can see by her various wins, I'd say it was a good idea. But as one of the greatest female swimmers of all time, she's just as lost as the rest of us. Endorsement deals, shiny medals and a name in the record books do not make it any easier. She too has only ever thought about swimming. Without giving everything she had, she felt she would not be as successful. It takes a commitment that very few people understand.

Rebecca realized she couldn't go back. She will never be as fast, as talented or willing to give her entire life to one thing. She

knew there had to be more. A diploma

from USC and cultured upbringing meant

she knew there was more to offer, but

what it is, she was unsure. She had

established the fact that a 9-5 work

schedule, coaching and being at a pool

were all unattractive options to her. She

defined herself as kind and hard working,

both things employers find desirable. But

where does that fit?

She felt pressure from herself and society

to be more. After being an idol in the

swimming world for so long, when she

said she's training to be a Pilates

instructor, she feels judgment and

questioning, much of which is self–inflicted. Rebecca began to wonder whether she's relevant or not. And all she wanted was to find passion and fulfillment and spend her days doing something that makes her happy. She told me, **"I don't need to be the best but I want to do what I love because I know what it feels like to do what you love, everyday."**

She missed the team aspect, and the ability to train next to a competitor, to share in victories and defeat and to feel the drive and energy pulse through her body each day. She didn't know how to workout just once a day. "I'm more motivated now than ever to workout three times a day to prove my relevance and ability. I want to know I'm still an athlete. But if I'm not currently training for a competition, what does that make me?"

She shared her fear of gaining weight, body image issues, how to make money once her brand becomes a thing of the past, and the difficulty of admitting weakness and a need for help. Rebecca knew she couldn't recreate the past, and although she knew this moment was always out there, it didn't make it any easier for her.

Rebecca joked with me suggesting I should finish the book as soon as possible so she could read it to gain some much needed insight. You'll see as The Transition goes on, in each athlete's story you will find an ability to relate, empathize and be amazed. Whether you are a high school athlete or one of the greatest of all time, you have the moment where you sit back and say to yourself, "Well, it's over… now what?" Rebecca was working on getting to the core. How will you do the same?

I am not defined by what I do, but by who I am.

Chapter 2

Dealing with Loss: the mourning period

"Retirement from football is like a social death and players have to be able to grieve the loss of football like a death. Until you're able to view it that way– because it's something we've done since we were kids– it's always going to be difficult." Life After the NFL: Typically a Struggle 4

We have all loved or been in love. I too, have loved. I had an absolute love affair with my sport. Call me crazy, but I am still secretly having it. It began the first time I smashed a ball to the ground, and to this day, every time I have one in my hands, I simply cannot let it go. It brings out butterflies, joy, pain, tears, memories and all the things you're supposed to have with an actual human. I spent countless hours, days, years, sleepless nights and beloved moments with this sport. It all ended so abruptly, and I just cannot seem to shake it. It calls to me every time I set foot in a gym.

"The relationship with sports created rhythm in life. As life changed, the pool was always the same. It was an anchor."
–Trent Staley, former USC Captain and NCAA Swimming Champion, USA National Team Member

When I retired, it was as if the love of my life had just died. I was depressed, felt lost and could not imagine anything ever filling that void again. What I did not realize at the time is that nothing could or ever will fill that void. My relationship with my sport is pure and perfect and a once in a lifetime kind of love. It stole a piece of my heart and will always have it. I learned a great deal and would not be anywhere near where I am today without it... so why try and replace it?

Please do not use this as relationship advice with your human romances– I'm no love guru. But I will say, I have had to mourn the after retiring. I had to say goodbye to a part of my life that was so significant and life changing. And it took me a long time. It is ongoing.

Every day I witness former athletes still holding on. They are not willing to let go, move on, or find peace. And in return, they are stuck reliving the dream and unable to find who they really are outside the "relationship." You have to allow yourself a mourning period. You cry, you get angry, you try to hold on, you relive all the memories, you go through the "what ifs" and the "maybe's", and then one day, you wake up, put on your pants, go outside, and become normal again; hopefully. One step at a time, you go on with your life. It

doesn't happen overnight, but allowing the

process to happen and keeping faith in

yourself will encourage you to "keep on

keepin' on," even when it seems hopeless.

Now, why is it so hard to move on? We

have touched on a few of the reasons so

far. First, it is your identity. You do not

know who you are without your sport.

Second, it's all you have known most of

your life. Your family has supported you as

the athlete, you have been practicing,

playing, studying for that sport almost

every day for years. Third, it is as if you

have lost the love of your life. You would

do anything for your sport; run sprints

until you puke, stay up all night watching film and live in a gym for ten years because you know that is what it takes.

A study conducted by David Lavallee and Hannah Robinson in 2006 revealed some insight on this very topic:

"Results revealed participants had been encouraged to dedicate their lives to gymnastics and were, as a result, left feeling lost and helpless when they retired. After prematurely adopting an identity based solely on their role as a gymnast, many of the participants knew little about who they were and what they wanted to do with their lives, and were consequently forced to distance themselves from their past in order to establish a new identity apart from gymnastics. For those who felt a constant external pressure to strive for excellence during their career, this process was particularly challenging and has lasted, in some cases, for the duration of their retirement. Distress can be avoided by engaging in pre-retirement planning from a very young age and

subsequently maintaining

control of the transition out of

gymnastics by reducing

participation gradually and

finding a meaningful

replacement." 5

As we distance ourselves and take a step

back, we realize there is even more loss

than just identity. We lose friendships. If

you are like me, you did not have an

exuberant amount of friends outside of

your team or sport because 99% of your

time was spent with them. So when it

came time to stop playing, you had to deal

with the evolution or loss of teammates

and relationships that had been consistent and strong for a long period of time. You may also come to the conclusion that you really had nothing in common with them outside of your sport and daily routine.

This was definitely difficult for me. I didn't really know where I fit in with everyone anymore. Luckily, my coaching staff was phenomenal and kept me involved. I went through phases in terms of spending time with my teammates and friends. There would be months where I was accepting and excited about that fact that they had 7am weights and I did not. Then there were times when I rebelled, said I hated volleyball and was out drinking with other friends until all hours of the morning. I was not really sure what to do or how to act so I just followed the emotions of the day.

Something that really helped me was finding a way to be involved without being involved. I was at matches, watching "my team" play, but I was calling the game for the web broadcast and interviewing them after. I still got to be there, and I was important in my new role. I'm not saying you should latch on and do what I did, but I do believe there is good in staying involved in some way. It makes the transition a bit smoother and there's nothing wrong with still being involved in your sport as long as you're taking the proper steps to move forward and find yourself. Putting a "band–aid" over it and expecting things to just be fixed is not the wise response. I have spoken with numerous athletes who competed at every level, and if there has been one clear message, it is that it **takes time to deal with this and most of them regret not getting to the root of their issues earlier**. At some point, we all have to accept where we are and learn how to take our experiences as an athlete and use them to help guide us in new directions. If you simply try and cover things up you are being unrealistic and unfair to yourself.

This is also why you see so many former athletes turn into coaches. Don't get me wrong, being a coach is an admirable job and I commend people who do it as it requires a lot of time, energy, knowledge, patience, and love for the game. There are a percentage of people who do coach because it has been their life's passion or a goal or career choice. Then there is a percentage who do it because they have no idea what else to do. Either way is fine, and I'm not saying it's wrong or judging it by any means. Again, I completely get it. It includes all things fantastic in the mind of a former athlete: control, competition, working out, routine, team and you get to live vicariously through the athletes. Don't we all want to live through the people who are doing what we want to? It's totally okay, but you have to come to terms with why you are doing something. Have you accepted your situation and have you dealt with it in a healthy way in order to continue to be around your sport and be this person? Or are you what I still am some days: A lost puppy who just wants to be 16 again and can't move on?

"Where else in the world do you get that camaraderie? Where you care more about the guys you play with than your own well-being and your own health. It's just a tight bond and an emotional attachment. It's family and then all of a sudden, it's gone. Just like that. You get into a feeling of 'I no longer belong.' That's devastating to a man." Mark Schlereth on Junior Seau 6

This next part is very serious and it breaks my heart to write about because it is so tough to talk about. But not enough people do and I feel an obligation to delve into this so that maybe we, as athletes and as fans, can help. A few people I deeply admire and respect were first to touch on these subjects, and rather than put it in my own words and shorten it, I felt it was necessary to include both of their articles, written so eloquently.

HONORING JUNIOR SEAU, by Dana Jacobsen

I didn't know Junior Seau the way his former teammates did or even some other members of the media. Come to think of it, whenever we spoke we were either rushing off a field, standing among a sea of reporters or talking via satellite, not exactly ways to build a personal bond. Still his suicide last week really stuck with me and it goes way beyond Seau himself.

We may never know why he took his life but I can't help but wonder what would have happened if he had just reached out for help instead of that gun.

In 9 and a half years at ESPN, I met a lot of former athletes. One question I'm pretty sure I always asked them at some point was about how they were adjusting to life away from the game. I can't think of a single one that didn't mention missing the "routine." That's probably not even a strong enough word for it. I mean this is a schedule of life that's been ingrained in most of them since childhood, at the very least from high school on. Imagine after all those years it's gone. How lost would you feel? I miss a couple days of my morning workouts or flip flop the time I'm on air for a week and it's like the life's been sucked out of me.

So if I'm aware of how big an adjustment leaving can be for these guys, don't you think the leagues they play for are aware too? A better question: what can they do about it?

The NFL and other pro sports leagues do their best to welcome the rookies in. From financial planning to warning guys about people who see them as prey, at the very least leagues offer advice and resources to their newest. What about the veterans? Why aren't there more resources for athletes who are leaving behind the only life they've ever known? There are no more OTAs or 2 a days, no playbooks to learn or team meetings to attend. The sport that's loomed larger than anything else in their lives, even family sometimes, is now just something they used to do to earn a living. I have to believe even the strongest man out there feels the impact of that.

I'm not saying this was the case for Seau. Again, I didn't really know him. I have heard speculation from some guys who did and we've all seen athletes struggle to varying degrees after leaving their sports behind. So why not help them make the transition? During collective bargaining we heard some talk about taking care of the veterans from a financial health standpoint and even physical health. What about mental health?

Yes it may be a taboo topic, but I'm going there. In a world full of strong men both physically and mentally, some may need help coping and that doesn't make them weak. Now as a gender, men seem to have a harder time asking for help than women. (Don't argue; just think about the pre-GPS days and who was more willing to ask for directions. Enough said.) So take that generalized male trait, add the machismo that goes with playing a sport like football and asking for help is not going to come easily. Help that is needed. Help leagues need to encourage, make accessible and destigmatize. 7

Mike Whitmarsh and the Plight of the Retired Athlete, by Bev Oden

On February 16, former AVP star and Olympic Silver medalist Mike Whitmarsh was found dead in a car inside a friend's garage. Two days later, the San Diego

County Medical Examiner's office ruled his death a suicide.

I don't know if he left a note or if anyone knows why he decided to take his own life. But I can't help but wonder if any part of the reason was what many retired athletes in this country struggle with – coping with life after sports stardom.

Mike Whitmarsh was one of beach volleyball's greats. He won 25 tournaments on the AVP tour (most with partner Mike Dodd) and took home $1.6 million in winnings over the course of his career. He lived the glamorous life of a pro beach player at the height of the sport's popularity. He retired after the 2004 AVP season and five years later he's gone.

The life of an elite athlete is a tough act to follow. After spending most of the formative years developing a natural talent and focused only on improving and dominating a sport, the great ones get to enjoy success and life at the top as one of the best in the country and possibly the world. The cheers, the respect, the accolades and the adoration become a part of daily life.

Actors, entertainers and rock stars can continue their craft well into old age. Clint Eastwood is still getting nominated for Oscars and the Rolling Stones are still filling arenas. But the human body is not equipped to compete at the top level of sports indefinitely. At some point, the body slows down, younger players start to challenge, and the once superstar athlete is forced to retire. The lights and the glamour fade out and are replaced with real life and its cubicles, fluorescent lighting and quarterly reports.

Is it any wonder that athletes have a tough time making the transition?

Maybe that's why so many once-great athletes un-retire after a few years out of the spotlight. Sure they're past their prime, but they can still compete on some level and may even find success again. The list of returnees is long – Michael Jordan, Magic Johnson, Brett Favre, George Foreman, Martina Navratilova, Jimmy Connors and Lance Armstrong just to name a few – but come-backs are short-lived and the athlete always winds up back in real life and often totally unprepared.

Where do all those years of dedication and gallons of sweat leave them when it is all over? While most have college degrees, their job has been playing their sport for the last 20 years. Many enter the workforce for the first time at 40+ years old with no real job experience to speak of.

Hopefully, they saved some of their money and can start their own business or foundation. Some land jobs in sports broadcasting or coaching. The rest find themselves searching for a place on the bottom rung of the ladder in a crowded job market. Suddenly the extraordinary become ordinary.

One former college athlete told me that he pursued a career in music after sports because he still longed to be applauded by a crowd. Real life has no equivalent. Some handle the loss of their former life better than others. They find an adequate job, raise children, settle in and move on. But many never quite find their way.

With the death of Whitmarsh, a wife is left without a husband, two girls are left without a father and the volleyball community mourns the loss of one of the great ones. Goodbye, Mike Whitmarsh. Rest in peace. 8

As interpreted from the previous two stories, Junior Seau and Mike Whitmarsh are two men that took their own lives because they just didn't know what else to do. Both were extremely famous, successful, admired legends in their respective sports. Now, no one can honestly say they know everything that went on. And I'm not here to speculate. What I am here to do is to take some responsibility and say, **we have to do better**. As fellow athletes, we have to look out for one another, remove the stigma and prevent these things from happening. We are a team, and we should help each other through The Transition.

"The way my career ended had an impact on me the first few years because I had no idea what to do next. It wasn't really until about three to four years ago when I really started to turn around and become more responsible about where I was and not being in this funk, in this depression and so forth," George said. "I was fighting demons and trying to get a peace of mind that did damage to me and my family, my wife. ... Hanging out and chasing [women] and all the wrong things." Former Titans Running Back, Eddie George

I sat down with my friend and colleague Curtis Conway, a USC sports legend and former NFL player (most notably with the Chicago Bears) to get his take on all of this. He is a man who comes from humble beginnings in Compton to a prestigious college, an outstanding 12 year NFL career and the same ending as the rest of us: completely lost and a wandering soul who wants nothing more than to replicate that feeling held so sacred to his heart. He said to me, **"Kelli, I wanted to die on that football field. To me, that was okay, because nothing else mattered. That was the dream, that's what I loved, and there was nothing else."**

This comment alone blew me away. As an athlete, I know what it means to love your sport. But to live and die for it? This is a feeling I didn't know. Or did I? We each manifest these feelings in different ways. Like the mourning of a death, as I have touched upon repeatedly, we each look at our sport differently and then deal with having to walk away in various ways. I played volleyball for 9 years. I lived it and breathed it, but as Curtis and I discussed, it wasn't my "everything." I knew I wanted more, to get into broadcasting and to pursue a different passion. And even with all that being said, I still struggled tremendously. Curtis faced the same predicament in his football career, which lasted 14 years longer than my volleyball career. Hailing from South Central, all he knew were drugs, gang banging, and famous black athletes, he realized he had only two ways out of that life. Get killed or be a stellar athlete. Curtis was blessed with immense talent and a drive that took him well beyond his wildest dreams. But while I was exposed to so many different dreams, careers, people and cultures, he didn't even know these things existed. So to die for football was not even a question. It was his reality, his only reality.

I asked him about talent. "How do we get these kids to realize there's more to them than their sport?" He said, "Some of them don't even know they have a talent." We can tell a kid they can write, act, sing, mentor, work with children, volunteer with homeless shelters, run a business, lead a discussion, yet they don't even know they can do these things. Exposure, upbringing, motivation, and sheer focus on one thing for so many years has given us all such tunnel vision that we don't even know who we are without our sport.

For some, from a young age, we are taught that sports are everything. Where do we get this mentality? In Chris Wagner's article "Pressure points," he describes the role childhood plays in our evolving attitude toward sports as we grow.

> "As a result, young players are distracted from learning, developing fundamental skills and having fun. Instead, kids

are learning that winning is everything and confrontation is the best way to achieve this success. Young athletes feel pressures from their parents other than the pressure to win. Many parents see success in athletics as a way to further the family name up the ladder of their community's social hierarchy. This will often cause brothers and sisters of successful older siblings to feel pressure to live up to their older siblings' accomplishments, not only in the eyes of their family, but in their schools and communities as well. A young child with low self-esteem and parents who have an unhealthy 'fixation on winning and losing' may become suffocated by the weight of carrying out these expectations. Parents of young athletes who are successful in the early years too often get the notion that their child can and will become a professional athlete. The pursuit of pro sports is a very noble quest. However, this decision should not be pressed onto a 10-year-old from his parents before even entering into the stage of puberty in which his size, weight, proportion and cognitive ability will drastically change."

The pressures become far too demanding and stressful, and although many athletes don't feel the effects at a young age, as post-career adults, it becomes all too evident for some. We (meaning athletes, parents and coaches) don't realize or forget to acknowledge the human element of it all. At the end of the day, regardless of physical ability, we all put our pants on the same way and we all have talents and passions just waiting to be ignited. Now is the time to accept that challenge. You're young and have the entire world at your fingertips. Will you replace the feeling playing your sport gave you? No. Curtis and I strongly agree that there will never be anything like this again. But you can find passion, spirit and talent in many other ways. It just takes a little time and a little patience. But I promise you it's there.

Finding an internship, career planning and networking were never things that entered Curtis' mind. They were complete afterthoughts, really. He was off to conquer the NFL. At least temporarily, his career path was set. Why waste time thinking about things that don't matter in this present moment? "I'm not there yet, I'm here to play. How can you tell me to focus on something else when I'm trying to give everything I have to football?" Fair question. We are taught from a young age to give 100% every day right? Practice, weights, games, film. If you don't give your all, you are a failure. But if everything you have is left on the field, what do you have left? How are you supposed to make time for something else? Well, to put it bluntly, "It's not an option to have another option." Curtis said this with such a sense of regret in his voice. He went on to tell me that he didn't think about the end until it started to creep up on him around years nine and ten of his NFL career. Then he realized he had no plan, no active network and no clue what to do. The problem, as he explained it, is that the Super Bowl ring on your finger doesn't mean much when you're 35 and sitting on the couch doing nothing every day. Is that what you've amounted to, in your entire life? I don't mean to sound harsh or unfair. I have deep respect for what that represents, and everything you put into it. But that's it? What about your other talents, passion and abilities? They're untapped and until you take the initiative to discover them, you may be depressed, lost and confused when it's all over. Why not be proactive?

What college students have to realize is it doesn't take that much extra time to meet with a career counselor, ask questions, and think about the future. Setting up another path can be as simple as answering the questionnaire I provided and talking to a counselor about what's available based on your interests. You take some meetings with donors or alumni from your school that are in those fields and get a sense for what it is like. And when you are ready, you have already done some of the dirty work. Now, of course you will have to go through The Transition and deal with all of the things talked about in this book, but at least you aren't starting from scratch. At least you've respected yourself, your intelligence and your future enough to do some planning.

Curtis went to the NFL after his junior year and didn't come back immediately to finish school. The story he told me about his return was very interesting. Mike Garrett, former athletic director of USC, had a conversation with Curtis when he was in school. Years later, this conversation sparked his interest to go back. Mr. Garrett said to Curtis, **"You don't take advantage of this school the way it takes advantage of you. You have all these resources and opportunities and you get nothing out of it because you don't even care."** We only see what's in front of us: the opportunity to play our sport. The schools use us to make money, gain prestige, whatever the reasons may be, and yet we walk away with empty hands outside of the competition. There is so much more. Why are we so one track minded that we never take advantage?

Every school, regardless of size, prestige and academic standards has so much to offer. Professors with years of experience and knowledge, successful alumni, meet and greets, guest speakers, networking events, internship and job fairs, career counselors, academic counselors, psychologists, nutritionists, physical therapists, doctors, bookstores, libraries and so on. Have you taken advantage of even just a few, on your own terms? (This doesn't include the vast majority of events you are forced to go to that you take nothing away from because all that matters is winning the next day.) We have so many opportunities, so many things available to us on a daily basis, and yet we choose to focus on something so singularly, when in reality, we can do more. We can take responsibility, see what is out there and use it to help guide our futures. If schools, player associations and professional leagues are going to spend money on resources to help athletes (especially when it comes to preparation and opportunities outside of your sport) then we should all be jumping on this. They can only do so much. Remember that saying, "you can lead a horse to water?" It is on us to close the deal. What are you waiting for?

Do more, be more, live more. Curtis and I wholeheartedly believe that planning earlier will keep friends from detaching from society, being miserable, lost, and even killing themselves. Doesn't it seem worth it to do a little more at 19 and 20 to eliminate some of this? You may not think you fall into this category, and I seriously hope you don't. **But the reality is so many people don't prepare themselves for life after sport and we sadly have to** personally experience and watch the demise of men and women once revered as, "The Greatest Ever."

Chapter 3

The struggle is real: developing your own
eating and sweating habits

"It can be a terrifying revelation when
who you are isn't who you were." ESPN's
Marty Smith from his article "How do
you cope when it's over?"

I found eating and working out to be really
difficult to get a grasp on during my
struggle. I have always been someone who
can eat a lot of food and workout and
maintain a strong, athletic figure. I am
blessed, thanks to my parents. But even
someone with good genes has to change
their routine in order to maintain a healthy

weight. The tricky part is not overcompensating. That is where I got into trouble.

I decided if I couldn't control my pain, depression or loss of volleyball, I would control what I ate. It became an obsession. Every day, I would read a diet book. I would limit myself to very few calories. Every single thing was fat free, sugar free, or light. I would drink insane amounts of flavored, calorie-free water and chew a pack of gum every day in order to fight the hunger pangs as well as trick my mouth into thinking I was eating. Writing these words makes me realize how outrageous these actions were. But at the time, it is all I knew. It is all I had left.

I had always been at a healthy weight my entire life. When I went home for Easter in 2008, my family and I were in church. I looked ill and sunken and I hardly had the strength to stand for the hour of mass. My mom kept yelling at me and I was extremely defensive. I knew what I was doing to an extent. The issue was that I did not realize why. My life was spinning out of control and all I had left was to control myself by eating rice cakes and fat free crackers.

After many comments from my mom, I finally went to see the athletic department's nutritionist, Kristy Morrell. Kristy had a lot of experience dealing with eating disorders. But the day I walked into her office, I had no idea what I was dealing with. We sat down for hours talking about not playing anymore, my disease and how I was feeling. She finally asked if she could tell me what she was seeing.

She saw a former athlete without any control, and my only way to cope was through food. I was in a state of shock. Kristy had to teach me how to eat all over again. It was a sign for what the rest of my life would be like– back to the basics.

I highly recommend meeting with the school or seek out a personal nutritionist. They will be able to structure a plan for you based on your needs and they take all the guesswork out of this process. But with or without a nutritionist, your golden rule should be this: Eat as many whole foods in their natural state as possible. Things that come in packages should be limited as much as possible. Jenna Phillips, the CEO and Founder of I AM ON A MISSION, a woman I truly admire and idolize for her approaches to nutrition and life always says: "Treat your body with love and care; you only get one." You did everything in your power to perform at the top level for your sport, so now the goal should be the same thing: fuel your body for the things you do now.

Okay, let's talk the sweat portion. It has been six years since I had to retire and I am still trying to figure out the right way to work out. This is not an easy thing. When I think about it, I've been taking orders from coaches and trainers since I was three years old. Swim, dance and soccer as a kid all the way through my second year of college. That's 16 years of structured workouts. If someone could explain to me how to work out after going through that for so long, I would be thrilled. The honest answer is, there is no "one size fits all" approach. Working out is different for everyone. Some people like to workout in the morning, some at night. Some like to lift weights and run sprints at Orangetheory, others like a nice easy pace on the treadmill and a Pilates class once a week. The most important thing is to find what works for you and stick to it. And also to remember, this will be an evolving, changing process every month.

I personally go through waves. Much of this has had to do with how my body is feeling so I have to react appropriately and listen to it. Often times, I lack the motivation. No one is waiting at the gym for me to show up. No one cares if I get in my cardio for the day. Now, it is all on me.

The best thing you can do is to find a routine as quickly as you can. Do what you love. Challenge yourself and make it a competitive environment. An athlete can't just turn off the competitive ego overnight, or ever in some cases. This is why I go to Orangetheory. A group environment makes me feel like I am on a team and I do my best to keep up or beat the person next to me. It makes a 7am workout a lot more fun and it leaves me with visions of summer workouts with the football team just as the sun was coming up.

"The hardest part of the transition has been finding alternative channels to express my competitive spirit in a healthy way. Finding a balance between completely shutting it off and still being active." -Donny Killian, former USA Junior National Team and Pepperdine/ USC Men's Volleyball

In Tomorrow's Trends article by Hannah Braime, she describes "5 Olympic Lessons A Business Can Learn About Competition." I believe that this not only pertains to the business transition but to athletics and competition in workouts as well.

Olympics and how they are a parallel for Business

There are strong parallels between what athletes strive for, endure, and achieve by getting to the Olympics, and the process an entrepreneur or business leader undertakes to reach the top of his or her field. Both worlds are highly competitive, both worlds are filled with the elite, and both worlds require the same level of grit and determination to reach the top. The athletes competing in the Olympics have already endured countless competitions to get to where they are today, just like business leaders.

Business leaders, entrepreneurs, and even employees who watch the Olympics can do well to explore and learn from the way athletes approach and manage competition - After all, it's the same process, just a different career field.

Business Motivators

Businesses and entrepreneurs have a choice: either they view competition as something to be feared and avoided, or they embrace competition, and use it to motivate and enhance their best work.

Businesses can only overcome competition by meeting it head on, yet so often failure starts internally. Self-doubt, external comparison and fear are all factors that cast a dark shadow over the benefits of competition. Olympic athletes are surrounded by the best in their field: they can either let themselves become overwhelmed by this, or let it inspire them to perform at a higher level. **Instead of being discouraged by competition, employees and business leaders need to turn their perspective on competition around, and use the anxiety that healthy competition induces to produce the best pitch, provide the best service, and be the best at what they do.**

CHAPTER 4

What else to expect: answering your most common questions

"Players always say the football field is a safe haven, that you can go there and block everything else out. But what do you do when that's gone and you have to deal with life? It can be a double-edged sword. I tell people all the time, you can retire from football. You can't retire from life." Derrick Brooks (Tampa Bay Buccaneers)

We have touched on eating disorders, suicide, and an overall identity crisis. Now, I hate to admit this, but that is not even close to being everything you can expect to deal with. Those may be the "umbrella" issues, but beneath each of those are all smaller issues that needle some of us until we feel like we are going crazy. Although the things I am about to describe seem trivial to non-athletes, you will find that these are the things that irk you the most.

Feeling withdrawn, like an outsider, and not fitting in.

As we grow up in sports, we belong. We are not outsiders because for most of us, being on a sports team provides a place where we can truly feel like ourselves. Everyone is like us. They are all on the same schedule, eat the same food at training table, wear the same sweats and talk about the same things. This is our normal, and this is all we know. Now take that away. What are you left with? You're left with what feels like nothing. On top of this, if you're like a majority of student-athletes, you only socialized with your "own kind," so when it comes time to not play anymore, you do not know anyone outside of this little bubble you have grown accustomed to.

I truly believe this is one of the main reasons we stick with our sport in the jobs we choose, beyond just wanting to be around it. What is the best way to get a job these days? Utilize your resources and the people you know. If the only people you know are volleyball coaches, players and parents, where on earth do you think you are going to end up? A job in volleyball or something relatively related is where we are the most comfortable. This is a space we don't necessarily have to expose ourselves to uncomfortable territories because we already know everything and everyone. Makes it pretty easy. I know I sometimes felt this way about my job as a volleyball analyst. I think it is great that I have been able to turn my volleyball career into a broadcasting career and I have been pretty smart about using my resources within the community to get ahead. Maintaining my relationships with the coaches, players, and networks that I grew up with has helped tremendously. But what happens when I am not in my volleyball bubble? Full blown panic sometimes. It gets really hard when you become irrelevant in a situation you are not an expert in.

The same goes for having friends outside of your sport. People tend to travel in packs or cliques. Athletes take this to a new extreme. When you are an athlete, at most schools, you live a VIP life. You have your own private building, locker room, training room, lounge, study hall, dining facility, and a travel schedule that takes you all over the country for a few months of the year. Unless you are in the Greek system or make a real effort to get to know your classmates, you are in a tough spot. It is not that you necessarily want this, but these are the people you are with and they also understand you.

The best way to handle it is to begin branching out. You cannot get to know other people until you get to know other people, so get out there. Internships and job related events are a great way to do this. Another great avenue is to utilize what your school has to offer. There are tons of alumni events, clubs, speaker series, and so on where you can go and get to know people outside of sports. A lot of the time, these are the well-connected, successful alumni who want to help you too, so it is a win-win situation for everyone. **Remember that many of these people are not athletes but want to be around and hire athletes so this is a great place for you to showcase all of your amazing talents.** Also, please understand I know these situations can be a bit awkward, and you are not necessarily going to feel like yourself. But getting out of your comfort zone creating relationships early on is what will matter in the long run.

You read Marcellus Wiley's story earlier about identity. But his plan of action had even more of an impact on me when we spoke.

If anyone knows relationships, it's this guy. When he was still in the NFL, he paid his cousin to cut and paste emails to everyone he met. He ended up receiving responses from everyone he reached out to and they were thrilled to interact with such an impressive athlete. He wanted to create bonds early because he knew that once his last game came, he'd need help moving on.

He began asking for advice and guidance from his contacts comprised of Columbia University Alumni, businesspeople, big time CEO's and everyone in between. He also turned to the man he calls his moral guide, Curtis Conway, for thoughts on the next steps.

Now, Marcellus says, the same people he sent emails to ten years ago are the ones who are first to help him network further, advance in his career and get involved in multiple projects. He told me, "No one wants to take the extra step. If you can't see your opponent and run through them, then you're a fake. You thought you were tough and thought you were the man. But when shit gets real, you get real."

Marcellus, I couldn't have said it better.

Now getting back to my point about being withdrawn. If you are in a situation like mine, and many others, where you have retired and were left to the side while everyone else continued playing, you have a very delicate situation on your hands. It's a natural reaction to retract, run away, and feel awkward with the people on your team. Not only do you not know how to act, but also, neither do they. The best thing to do is to only let this stage last for a short period of time. Those are your friends, so be friends with them. You will find that you have less in common with them than you once did. It is natural to move on and not want to talk about tennis all day long when you're not playing. But I urge you to have a frank conversation with people. Let them know how you feel. Tell them you are sad, you feel weird, and that it is hard to watch them go to practice every day while you are twiddling your thumbs trying to figure out what to do with the eight hour chunk of time that is now available to you. I found when I communicated with my teammates and friends and expressed my concerns, they were totally understanding and happy that I shared. It is when you are quiet and not answering texts and calls for days on end that things get rocky. The whole point of this book is to open up the lines of communication, so this is no longer a taboo topic. We are here to help each other. If you do not say how you feel, how is your teammate going to realize what's happening to you and what will (because it WILL) happen to them. This is your obligation.

This leads me to the next issue: time management. People have been scheduling your life for years. You have probably only had to think about how to write a five page paper in two hours the night before it is due. Between mandatory study hall, classroom checks, plane rides, and hotel time, you have most likely been booked solid but also able to manage it all. Someone says jump, and you say "how high?" Now, it is on you. When to wake up, study, eat, sleep, workout, party– it is all up to you. You see most seniors in their second semester attempting to live how "the other side" has been living for three and a half years... wake up at noon, grab coffee and a burrito, maybe make it to class, then go home, nap, eat dinner and pre party before the big Thursday night rage at your favorite bar.

Most athletes I have spoken to share this as one of their main concerns. Without weights, film, practice and study hall, what are you supposed to do? Enjoy yourself, that's what! Easier said than done, but eventually this is the goal. To learn how to be an adult, make your own decisions and decide how you want to live your life. Athlete or not, that's what your late teens and early twenties are for. So, once you're done, I would give it a little time. But don't get caught up in a lazy lifestyle. It is unhealthy and doesn't create good habits. It's also very easy to get sucked into and much harder to get out of. **You have been disciplined as an athlete for however many years now; be sure to use that now.** Find out what you like and go with it. Maybe you have never had a chance to figure that out, so do just that. Take the time to figure it out. There's no right or wrong here; it is what is best for you. (Do you hear that? YOU get to do what YOU want. I know this is a bizarre concept, but it's something you will learn to love. You're your own boss, motivation and guide. Rise to the challenge.) But you have to put in the work to figure it out. Do yourself a favor though; do not lose the workouts, relatively early wake-ups or bed times. **You will realize a routine is about productivity and the key to all of this is to feel good**. Working out keeps you healthy. Do not deny the important things.

Regardless of sports, this is a time in all of our lives when we start making decisions as to what we take seriously, what we spend our time on, and what we turn away from. Ask yourself: How do I want to spend my time? What really brings me joy? Maybe you know what these things are already. But if you are like most young people, you have yet to have the talk with yourself.

So I challenge you to ask yourself these questions, write down every answer that comes to mind and then go back and question yourself as to why you chose these things. You will surely find that what you think matters to you, probably doesn't. So much of what we choose to spend our time and focus on is trivial or for other people. Dig deep within yourself. Because once you have a real conversation about what matters most to you, you can begin to understand who you are at the core and where to go now that your sport doesn't rule your life. **To thine own self, be true.**

Getting lost in what could have been. I could have been an All-American. I could have been more. What would have happened if they had just let me have the opportunity? Even those of you that were All-Americans, Olympians, starters, and MVPs know the feeling of wanting more for your career and never seeing it come to fruition.

This is a big reason why people continue to play far past their prime. They are waiting for their moment, for their big accolade. For some, it comes. For most though, it doesn't. And when we are done playing our sport, we are left chasing the "what if" forever.

A lot of people go on to fulfill this as a coach and many people step away from their sport just to come back to it after a certain period of time to see "if they've still got it." Unfortunately, it's usually the same outcome... falling short of the grand expectations. Trent Staley, former USC and USA swimmer said to me one day, **"Sports have a 100% failure rate."** We are left with an unfulfilled, empty feeling. We will always be the kid that wanted to score the home run or be cheered on by thousands

after winning a National Championship.

These visions will haunt us. And will come

out to bite us in every facet of our lives;

work, relationships, etc. This will be both

an emotional struggle and internal battle.

How do we stop this and keep it from

taking over? Let go of the control and

living in the "what-ifs". As much as I wish

this were not true, if this book tells you

anything, it is we don't have control over

much. The moment we come to this

realization and accept that everything

happens as it is supposed to and that

some people are not meant to have the

shining moment we all believe we deserve,

that is when we can begin to heal. And

even more so, have you ever asked yourself the reason why you never had that moment that was supposed to make it all worth it? Why would that moment have made it all worthwhile? Why was your career cut short by a torn ACL? I am a firm believer in everything happening for a reason. What's your reason and what are you learning from it?

Travis Hannah, former Trojan and NFLer is speaking out after many years of silence. He finally feels comfortable talking about his dark, twisted journey and his relationship with football. Although I had been previously told about his experience, I didn't believe it until he walked me through each moment, each thought, and the permanent mark it left on his life.

From Hawthorne, California, the inner city athlete found his way to USC with best friend Curtis Conway. After a successful college career, Travis was one of the lucky ones to make it to the NFL. He thought he had it made. The life, the prestige, every kid's dream. But after just three years, the dream was over and life as he knew it would never be the same.

"I sat on the couch in Houston by my phone for four straight years, just waiting for a team to call me. The call never came," he told me. "I couldn't go out in public, I went grocery shopping late at night so no one would see me. I was so embarrassed and ashamed. I thought everyone was judging me and was completely paranoid." On that couch, Travis would eat alone, talk to himself, separate himself from society completely, and eventually get alopecia, (the partial or complete absence of hair from areas of the body where it normally grows; baldness) brought on by severe stress and anxiety, which caused him to lose all the hair from his body.

"I couldn't handle being on center stage and then becoming just a regular part of society. It was a culture shock. I started questioning myself– what if I had done more? I became delirious. I was in a deep depression."

After those four years, Travis' mom called Curtis Conway and another friend to go out to Texas to rescue Travis from himself. The two flew out and brought him home to Los Angeles. "I got home, looked at myself, and when I watched my mom looking at me, I realized I looked like a different person. I finally understood just how bad it was."

Travis began to pray for guidance. His prayers were for purpose and a clear path to begin again. After some time at home, getting back to his roots, he felt he was most helpful to society working with kids. It gave him purpose and fulfillment and he found he could impact kids and provide a strong male role model that he unfortunately never had.

"No one raised me to think about life after sports. No man was there telling me how to invest, to think about the bigger picture, or realize I have more to offer. I want to make sure these guys understand it all ends, at one point or another, and I want them to learn from my mistakes. No one told me, but I will share my story to protect them. I hit rock bottom, but they don't need to."

Travis continues to tell his story to change the outcome for the new generation of athletes. His coaching has bred young men that are successful beyond sports. Many have found careers in the NFL front offices, own their own clothing lines and attend Ivy League universities. The real conversation, the truth and the ability to share are what Travis and I believe make all the difference in how The Transition is made.

CHAPTER 5

The Game Plan: the little details make the most impact

"It is important to create a climate wherein people have an opportunity to be heard, which will ultimately allow for the truth to be heard." Dr. Christina Rivera, Associate Athletic Director, Academic and Student Services, UCLA

Sometimes, it is tough to ask for help. Most athletes are self- sufficient, go-getters who know what they need to do to win, and they go do it. They are arrogant, prideful people who do not want to ever admit weakness. Unfortunately, this is not something you can get through alone, and this is not a time to be prideful. It is a time to be vulnerable, communicative and willing to fight the hard fight.

In the Journal of Excellence's article, "Life After Sport: Athletic Career Transition and Transferable Skills," it states "Currently, there are significant organizational obstacles to the proper treatment of career transition difficulties for athletes (Taylor & Ogilvie, 1998). Many athletes have limited contact with qualified sport psychologists, which is problematic for athletes trying to access professional help when transitioning out of sport (Taylor & Ogilvie). Alternatively, athletes may not perceive counseling as an important

component of their career transition. For

instance, Sinclair and Orlick's (1993)

research details that former world-class

amateur athletes indicate they did not view

individualized counseling to be a helpful

coping strategy when transitioning out of

sport. Improving athletes' access to

competent counselors and building a

strong therapeutic relationship are the

essential first steps.

General Goals

The general goals for treatment, in

relation to athletes transitioning out of

sport, are to create a more successful

positive transition and to increase

awareness of transferable skills in order to make effective life changes.

Two primary factors may aid in this endeavor: a) emotional well-being and b) use of transferable skills. Counseling professionals can play a key role in helping to create successful transitions for athletes. Counselors and counseling interventions can assist athletes as they cope with the emotional impact of transitioning (Danish, Petitpas & Hale, 1992)."

Your mentality, attitude and lifestyle will change dramatically. Because of the way this will impact your inner being, you will want to seek out those that can help guide you through. Now, each situation is very different. You need to find what works best for you. But I beg of you, do not keep it to yourself. That's by far the worst thing you can do. That is what most athletes do and the following can happen: addiction, suicidal thoughts, withdrawal from social activities, loss of friends and family, loss of identity, weight gain, weight loss, depression... the list goes on. Respect yourself enough to realize people want to help you. But **you** must seek them out. I am sure people in my life are tired of hearing me talk about The Transition. But it is like this secret life I led for years that I can finally talk about and now. The moment I moved from silence to communication, my head, heart and soul opened up and I could finally relate with others in the same place and the wounds could begin to heal. It has been incredibly empowering.

Your first stop, whether you are currently competing or have already finished, should be your family and friends. You are going to need their support, mentally and emotionally, and the only way they are going to know how this is affecting you is if you tell them. **What most people fail to realize is that people who were never athletes fail to understand this process.** They do not realize there is a grieving process. For some athletes, there is a void and pain after playing has ended, so if you don't express your feelings, they will have no idea what is going on. By having this conversation early, you also help yourself begin to cope and accept the situation. This way you do not avoid reality and you find solace in being able to communicate and feel support, sympathy, or whatever is most needed.

"There's no easy transition. I don't care if you play 50 years or have a farewell tour. It doesn't hurt any less. Call it narcissism. Maybe. But it's the damn truth. And it's scary." Brad Daugherty, NBA

This conversation can begin very simply:

"Family and/or friends, I feel

_____

_____ now that I am not playing

anymore. I miss _____ and I

need help with

_____. I

don't know how to handle

_____ and I

wake up every morning thinking about

_____. I need

you guys to

_____

so that I can get through this."

These thoughts will probably summarize most of your "big feelings." From here, you can begin to get into the little issues: Why do you feel this way? How does it impact your daily life? There are steps you can take to gain normalcy again. You need sounding boards and people that can step in and be your support system.

"I was looking for anything to grab onto for comfort. I think I would have done better coping with the difficulties if my team and family had been more supportive. I felt like I was losing my entire identity and worth and I felt like a failure when I was rejected from the

swimming world." Megan Wheeler,

former USC Swimmer

Next up, sports psychologist. Now, I can

literally feel you cringing just reading

those words. I appreciate being able to

talk things out. Sometimes it's hard to

admit my flaws, mistakes and problems

but I walk out of there with a clear mind

and heart and with tools to take on life's

obstacles. Had I not begun psychology

immediately after retiring, I know I would

still be a disaster today. Not only are these

people taught how to handle these

situations, but they also have the ability to

walk you through your feelings, give

meaning to the things you don't

understand and provide answers for your questions about who you are and where you're going. And the best part is, you can say anything you want and they won't judge you, criticize you or run and tell your friends. It was my room of trust, support and realistic guidance and I was able to navigate my way through my feelings and come out so much happier and at peace. As mentioned previously, I urge you to put your pride aside and be willing to ask for help. The more you open up, the more you heal and the more fulfilling your life can be. So do not wait, do not think, just do. I promise you will be glad you did it.

"Those who hold it in will only struggle at some point in their life, when all that they have hidden comes out." Jerritt Elliott, Head Coach University of Texas Women's Volleyball, 2012 National Champions, AVCA Coach of the Year

If you are still a student, meet with your academic advisor. I'm guessing most people reading this book were focused on sports, so academics and careers were an afterthought. That is why most people struggle with The Transition. They stop playing and then they say, "Well, what am I supposed to do now?" Strategizing with classes and studies is a great first step. What are you studying? Do you even like it?

What is it you are doing now that sets you up for what is next? Academic advisors can help you structure a plan to help you get where you want to go. Ideally, this is a conversation you should have the minute you step foot on campus. But it is never too late. If you are not studying what you want, find out what you can do to make some changes. Often times we forget it is not all about the major or classes we have in college that determine our career. What matter more are the hands-on experiences in the workplace. So after you speak with your advisor, head over to the career counselor.

On the next page is a questionnaire I believe will be extremely helpful for you. It outlines your "Dream Job" to help point you in the direction best suited for your personal aspirations. Answer these and use it as a tool to begin your new path. Find an internship, get experience and allow the career counselor to help you do all of this. They're experts at creating a path and deciphering what would be your best fit. Use them! Companies LOVE hiring athletes. Many have good work ethics, are competitive, outgoing, strong willed, smart, strategic, multi-taskers. These represent marketable qualities companies are looking for in job candidates.

"I realized a lot of athletes didn't know what they wanted to do after graduating. I felt like we needed a meaningful way to use the skills we developed as players– focus, teamwork, persistence, and dedication– to help others. I wanted to show other athletes that sports teach you a lot of intangible life skills you can use to pursue life goals outside of sports." Parker Goyer, former Duke Tennis star, current charity star

Dream Job

We all have a dream job in mind. For some of us, friends and family also have a vision of what we should become. The idea behind this exercise is to get you to turn off all the voices of people who are telling you what you should and should not do and think about what YOU want to do with the rest of your life.

These questions are designed to stimulate thought about a 'wish list' for a dream job. It will also get you to think about your current internship and evaluate the experience in comparison to your 'wish list.'

1. How will you define success? (money, status, power, influence, balance, other)
2. Do you have a role model for success?
3. What is your dream job title?
4. Where are you while doing the work of your dream job? (outside, inside, large office, cubicle)
5. What do you wear to work?
6. Who are your colleagues? Describe the type of people you will give you energy and motivate you to succeed.
7. Who is your boss? What is he/she like? Or are you your own boss?
8. How many hours do you work each day?
9. How are you compensated for your work?
10. How do you get to work? How long does it take?

11.What do you do for fun?
12.Who or what influences your choice of work?
13.How important is work/life balance in your choice of career?

Now take a minute to think about 'fit' in an organization.

1. What do you admire in people who you view as successful?
2. Can you develop a list of 4–5 values that must be present in the work ethic of your employer?
3. What would convince you to accept a job offer?
4. What would end a negotiation and have you walk away from a job offer?
5. How long are you willing to wait to achieve your dream job?

Once you have completed the Dream Job questionnaire, you should have a better idea of the direction you're looking to go. Now the idea of branding comes into play. Why, you ask? Think about this for a moment. You are a brand already. Joe, the athlete, is a brand on its own. Now we must redefine Joe's brand. By redefine, I do not mean get rid of the current brand, but rather redefine to suit his current needs as well as those of his new audience (the employer).

In "IT'S TIME TO BRAND YOURSELF" by Blaise James, the Gallup Global Brand Strategist, he says, "Your personal brand must be authentic, of value to your boss, and aligned with your company's goals. What's more, your personal brand should be more than an elevator speech, self-help jargon, or a couple of positive corporate buzzwords." This is why it is so important to break down what your greatest dreams and aspirations are, who you want to be, and where you are going. You must define this yourself before you can share it with someone else.

The article states, "You already are a brand, whether you know it or not. Your bio, experience, skills, behaviors, appearance, even your name—they all express your brand. What you need is a clear brand strategy– just like good corporations strive for– to make sure you are portraying yourself in a way that achieves your objectives... **Your purpose, your point of view, and your principles —three key components of your brand— are about more than just your job;**

they're integral to your career and life.
You want to have your long-term strategy
nailed down so that your tactics are as
effective as they can be."

Branding and presenting yourself in the
best light is highly important online with
social media and networking. When using
sites such as LinkedIn, understand this is
the perfect place to present yourself in a
more formal, put together, "look why I'm
so hirable" manner. You want to list your
internships, volunteer work, and objectives
so employers can see a clear picture of
who you are and where you'd like to be
with one click. Your picture should be
professional and visible.

As we talk about branding, it is vital to discuss your physical presentation. It was interesting asking employers what they want out of potential candidates. I got the "run of the mill" answers, but then one struck me that pertained specifically to athletes: their style. I had honestly never thought about what role fashion played in a potential employment setting. Obviously you want to look professional. But Trent Staley, who now heads Marketing at Nascar said this is one of the most important things to him. We both laughed as we talked about living in sweats all through college and rarely putting on a nice outfit. So when he sees potential employees now, he wants to see if they have their own sense of style and are able to play the dual role of comfortable athlete and sassed up businesswoman. Be your own person and dress the way you want to be represented. It's part of your brand.

Now, we need to turn our focus to meeting with potential mentors, bosses, or networks. I take a lot of meetings with young guys and gals in college or those who just graduated that want to get into broadcasting. Like I said earlier, I have had incredible mentors and help along the way, and I am excited to pay it forward and answer questions for everyone. That is the only way this business works correctly.

I am always interested to see a few things: do they confirm our meeting, how do they communicate (text, email, call), how do they dress, how early are they, how prepared are they to talk, do they bring something to take notes with and do they send a follow up thank you email after?

A couple different examples: I met with a current-student athlete who wanted to know about how to get into the entertainment television world. Although this is not my specialty, I had a brief stint at E! News and have formed my own opinions about that aspect of the business. And after all, television is television and the networks of people cross over so I was happy to chat about it. This young woman sent me a text message to initiate the meeting, confirmed with me and showed up in nice sweats to our coffee shop meeting. Not a problem, I was in jeans and a t-shirt and I realize she is between practices. But here's the kicker, no note pad and no sense of what to ask. Here's where my concern comes in to play. If you have no idea what you want and have not researched the field, potential employers or have some semblance of what to talk about, why will someone want to sit down with you? So the conversation was choppy and less helpful than it could have been. I will not necessarily offer information if I am not asked about it.

Young people tend to struggle with receiving a ton of information at once at an already overwhelming time of their lives, so if I don't feel they are prepared to delve deeper, I won't lay out all the cards. I feel it out and try to do my best. Long story short, this girl never ended up pursuing anything in this field, which is completely fine, but maybe had she been ready and able to ask more questions, she would know more about what it was she wanted to get into. And that is where passion is different than interest.

Passion. I saw passion from my next meeting. I received a very professional and seriously toned email from a former college football player, complete with a resume, description of interests and what he hoped to gain from meeting me. He was trying to get into the broadcasting world and wanted to pick my brain. We were the same age and he as well as our mutual friend thought it would be helpful. So I took the meeting. We were set for dinner at a restaurant and as he walked in, I saw a very well dressed man, in a suit with perfectly groomed hair join me at the table. He shook my hand and was very ready to ask questions. In his mind, he had the entire conversation scripted to gain every possible piece of advice. This was impressive and you can clearly see how very different the scenarios are. First impressions mean everything, so do not take lightly how early you show up, how well prepared you are, and your ability to be passionate about the topic at hand. Remember, these people are doing you a favor. Show respect and humility at all times and be sure to show your appreciation.

As you begin to reach out to your network and ask for informational meetings with people, Eileen Kohan, my Career Counselor during my days at SC, always reminded me to put it in your own words and add your personality. The former college football player is very serious, direct and uber professional person in his emails. I, on the other hand, like exclamation points and smiley faces. Maybe not on the first email but I like to lay it out there for people and show them who I am from day one. It makes me feel more comfortable. You have to find the language that suits you best. See the example below.

Dear John Smith,

I recently met with my advisor Linda Jackson about my future endeavors post-graduation and she mentioned that you would be the perfect person to meet with regarding career opportunities in advertising. I'm in my junior year at USF and am currently majoring in Business. I've been extremely interested in learning more about account management and design and would appreciate 30 minutes of your time to learn about the field.

Please let me know if you have free time to meet either in person or by phone in the next two weeks. I look forward to our conversation.

Best,

Jane Williams

USF Women's Tennis Team

555.686.9578

Or if you already know this person from a previous relationship and have yet to ask them for help, the following can work:

John,

Hope things are well! I thought of you as I began researching internships and possible career paths once I've completed my degree requirements. You have spoken so highly of your company and advertising in general, and I was hoping to spend some time getting to know more about it and see if it would be a good fit for me. It's always been something that has piqued my interest but I'd really like to dive deeper and get a better sense of the industry. Let me know if you have some time, I would really appreciate it. Thanks so much!

Best,

Jane Williams

USF Women's Tennis Team

555.686.9578

Remember, employers love to hire athletes. I reached out to a former Notre Dame Women's Softball player, Linda Kohan, for her guidance. She is a 25-year-old working in private wealth management for Goldman Sachs in Chicago. She is personally in charge of recruiting interns from Notre Dame. Linda said she looks for the following traits in candidates: hard working, smart, able to converse, ability to show interest and/or find answers (research), confident, coachable, able to earn respect and trust. She said, "embrace the fact that your whole life has been a job and learn how to spin it into normal life." She was able to do just this by using her aggressive, competitive nature in the workplace. Although intimidating to be in wealth management at such a young age, Linda found a way to use her greatest assets of leadership and problem solving to push the boundaries, speak up for herself and propose improvements on projects to her colleagues. Linda also added how important it is to "have passion rather than interest." We can all show interest in something, but if you bring the type of passion you had for your sport to your new workplace it will be evident you are willing to go above and beyond because you believe in not only the end result, but the process as well. Games are important but practices get you where you need to be. **If you don't bring the fire every day, Saturdays just don't matter.**

I had a chance to talk with a young woman recently who I've known since we were ten years old. We were rivals throughout our careers, through college and then she went on to play professionally and with the US National Team. From a very young age,

Cynthia Barboza was anointed "Volleyball's Golden Child," and not by herself. The entire Southern California community as well as USA Volleyball decided this was her gift, her future, and that was it. Now that's great, and I was of course always jealous of her talents and accomplishments. But in Cynthia's mind, she never made that choice for herself, and quite frankly had far more to offer than her ability to crush a ball down the line. Cynthia speaks multiple languages, has a diploma from Stanford University and in my opinion, is one of the brightest and most eloquent women I know. She described to me how frustrating it has always been, and even more so now as she has just ended her 15 year playing career, to deal with everyone else's expectations and dreams for her. **"People don't even know me. People I thought were great friends… they have no idea who I am. And they keep calling this a phase. It's not a phase, and I am not volleyball. I never was. They just kept telling me I was."**

As you continue to prepare yourself for more opportunities, below is a great way to make the most of your internship:

MAKING THE MOST OF YOUR INTERNSHIP EXPERIENCE

An internship should provide the following opportunities in most situations:

1. Work on a specific project with a designated manager.
2. Either "formal" or "on the job" training.
3. Include rotational assignments through different departments to gain an understanding of the big picture of an organization's operation.
4. Provide performance feedback and mentoring.

STEPS TO CREATING A SUCCESSFUL INTERNSHIP EXPERIENCE

1. How will this move you toward your career goal?

2. Schedule a formal appointment with your supervisor to establish goals for your projects.

3. Learn the organization structure. Who has the decision making power? How are decisions made?

4. You probably have a lot of good ideas on how you could do things better. Introduce those ideas at appropriate times when you will be heard. Your credibility is critical to your success.

5. Always be proactive and offer to do more tasks or shadow someone.

6. Network! Network! Network!

ADVICE:

Pretend you're playing your sport. How would you conduct yourself?

1. Always show initiative, no matter how menial the task at hand may seem to be.
2. Ask questions. Start with the basics. Make mistakes.
3. Take ownership. Take initiative. Be confident in what you are doing. Don't be shy!
4. Be open to criticism, have an open mind and ask questions.
5. Don't be intimidated by your lack of knowledge.

The last person I feel plays an incredibly important role in The Transition is a mentor. This person is different than family, friends and counselors. A mentor guides you from a standpoint of personal experience and can provide you with insight and ideas on how to handle your many issues. I am lucky enough to have many mentors; some within USC athletics, some in the broadcast industry, and parents of friends. Each mentor in my life is incredibly influential. They are people who I deeply trust, respect and admire for different reasons. They come from various backgrounds and see me for who I really am. Without personal desires getting in the way, they provide me guidance that is true to who I am and the goals I have shared with them, both present and future. This allows me to see myself from many angles and stay on the path most important to me. They are people who can say what I need to hear, but most of the time, give it to me straight, in a way filled with love and support. Besides my psychologist, these people continue to play the most vital roles in my transition.

The Harvard Business Review Outlines Mentorship as the following:
Make mentoring personal: Demonstrate your investment in their success by asking what kinds of work they want to do, where their passions lie, and what skills they want to develop.

What makes a Mentor:

1. Someone absolutely credible whose integrity transcends the message, be it positive or negative

2. Tells you things you may not want to hear but leaves you feeling you have been heard

3. Interacts with you in a way that makes you want to become better

4. Makes you feel secure enough to take risks

5. Gives you the confidence to rise above your inner doubts and fears

6. Supports your attempts to set stretch goals for yourself

7. Presents opportunities and highlights challenges you might not have seen on your own

Many schools have mentor programs in place you may not know about. Your academic advisor and coach are great places to start to try and locate such a program. If there is not a current program, ask if there are any alumni involved in the athletic department still that would be willing to work with you. Or maybe you know someone through your major or an event that could help you with the transition. There are no guidelines for who a mentor needs to be. It just needs to be someone you trust, have or can build a relationship with, and someone who is connected to who you are and where you want to go. And if they have gone down the path you just so happen to currently be on (emotionally, mentally, career-wise) then slam-dunk for you!

When I mentor student athletes, I ask the following questions, which I recommend you to use:

1. What is it about this specific career path that you like?

2. What else falls in the same category but maybe a different career path? i.e. public relations for sports, entertainment, news

3. What don't you like about the idea of this career?

4. Who do you already know in this field that you can reach out to? (If

you have already talked to them, the next step is to urge them to help you find an internship.)

5. What jobs are out there that fit with your interests and specific expectations? (If you do not know the answer to this, this is where the career counselor comes in)

Mentors are hands on, helpful, constructive, organized, good at listening and creating opportunities. They also lend an ear and a heart to their mentees. They are relatable and an open book. Mentors hear the athlete, accept what they are saying or feeling, and provide insight into the bigger picture.

As you take someone through The Transition, understand what that means. Baxter Magolda's Theory of Self-Authorship outlines what happens during this time of "crossroads."

Baxter Magolda defines self-authorship as "the internal capacity to define one's beliefs, identity, and social relations" and answers the three following questions (Evans et al., 2010, p.184).

How do I know? Who Am I? How do I want to construct relationships with others?

Four phases toward self-authorship:

- Phase 1: Following Formulas—allowing others to define who you are, "young adults follow the plans laid out for them" while assuring themselves they created these plans themselves (p.185)

- Phase 2: Crossroads—The plans a student has been following do not necessarily fit anymore, and new plans need to be established. Students are dissatisfied with self. As student development professionals, we should be extremely adept at seeing this stage and know how to guide our students to a life of purpose when they are at the "crossroads."

- Phase 3: Becoming the Author of One's Life—creating the ability to choose own beliefs and stand up for them (especially when facing conflict or opposing views)
- Phase 4: Internal Foundation —"grounded in their self-determined belief system, in their sense of who they are, and the mutuality of their relationships" (p. 186)

In order to develop a strong internal foundation, students need to trust the internal voice and build an internal foundation.

How does this apply to student development professionals? Students who worked with advisors who encouraged reflection in goal setting and intentional planning and discussed with students their nonacademic life experiences were more likely to develop abilities and perspectives associated with self-authorship" (Evans et al., 190).

"The most successful student-athlete is the humble learner." -Christina Rivera, UCLA

It is up to you to make the most of your Transition. Embrace this opportunity, much like you did on your first practice of your last season of competitive play. Go

for it!

I'd like to thank the following people, for

helping make this book possible:

Evan and Martha Olson

Mike Voight, Phd.

Christina Rivera

Eileen Kohan

USC Sports Psychology Dept.

The countless athletes named throughout this book, and those from anonymous interviews, for your transparency and courage. Your words are what make this possible.

To my parents, Steve and Viviana, and incredible younger brother Steven, thank you for getting me through The Transition. You are my rocks and inspiration and I would be lost without your constant compassion and kind hearts.

Sources

1. Leslie Myer. Nancy K Schlossberg's Transition Theory. http://cspcompetencyportfolio.weebly.com/uploads/1/4/5/6/14568912/formal_theory_paper_6020.pdf Accessed November 25, 2013.

2. Leslie Myer. Nancy K Schlossberg's Transition Theory. http://cspcompetencyportfolio.weebly.com/uploads/1/4/5/6/14568912/formal_theory_paper_6020.pdf. Accessed November 25, 2013.

3.   Marty Smith. How do you cope when it's over? http://espn.go.com/racing/ nascar/cup/story/_/id/7916568/ nascar-marty-smith-athletes-die- twice. Accessed November 25, 2013.

4.   William J. Price. What are the odds of becoming a professional athlete? http://www.thesportdigest.com/ archive/article/what-are-odds- becoming-professional-athlete. Accessed November 25, 2013.

5.   Alejandro Bodipo-Memba. Life After the NFL: Typically A Struggle. http:// usatoday30.usatoday.com/sports/ football/super/2006-01-28- retirement-perils_x.htm. Accessed November 25, 2013.

6. David Lavallee and Hannah Robinson. In Pursuit of An Identity: A Qualitative Exploration of Retirement from Women's Artistic Gymnastics. http:// core.kmi.open.ac.uk/display/ 9549106. Accessed November 25, 2013.

7. Marty Smith. How do you cope when it's over? http://espn.go.com/racing/ nascar/cup/story/_/id/7916568/ nascar-marty-smith-athletes-die- twice. November 25, 2013.

8. Dana Jacobson. Honoring Junior Seau. http://danajacobson.blogspot.com/ 2012/05/honoring-junior-seau.html. Accessed November 25, 2013.

9. Beverly Oden. Mike Whitmarsh and The Plight of The Retired Athlete. http://volleyball.about.com/b/2009/03/19/mike-whitmarsh-and-the-plight-of-the-retired-american-athlete.htm. Accessed November 25, 2013.

10. Chris Wagner. Pressure Points. http://www.cpyu.org/Page_p.aspx?id=77250. Accessed January 1, 2014.

11. Marty Smith. How do you cope when it's over? http://espn.go.com/racing/nascar/cup/story/_/id/7916568/nascar-marty-smith-athletes-die-twice. November 25, 2013.

12. Hannah Braime. 5 Olympic Lessons A Business Can Learn About

Competition. http://
www.tomorrowstrends.dev.perfection
coding.com/health-business/5-
olympic-lessons-businesses-can-
learn-about-competition.html.
Accessed June 1, 2013.

13. Jeffri Chahhida. Life After NFL a
Challenge For Many. http://
espn.go.com/nfl/story/_/id/
7983790/life-nfl-struggle-many-
former-players. Accessed May 5,
2013.

14. Kerbi McKnight, Kerry Bernes, Thelma
Gunn, David Chorney, David Orr and
Angela Bardick. Journal of Excellence.
Issue 13. Life After Sport: Athletic
Career Transition and Transferable

Skills. https://www.uleth.ca/dspace/
bitstream/handle/10133/1175/
Life_After_Sport.pdf?sequence=1.
Accessed July 3, 2013.

15. Marty Smith. How do you cope when
it's over? http://espn.go.com/racing/
nascar/cup/story/_/id/7916568/
nascar-marty-smith-athletes-die-
twice. November 25, 2013.

16. Colleen Oakley. Parker Goyer aces her
next act. http://espn.go.com/espnw/
journeys-victories/6893269/former-
duke-blue-devils-tennis-star-
parker-goyer-aces-act. Accessed
June 1, 2012.

17. Blaise James. It's time to brand
yourself. Gallup Business Journal.

http://businessjournal.gallup.com/ content/121430/time-brand- yourself.aspx. Accessed April 1, 2010.

18. Amy Gallo. Demystifying Mentoring. Harvard Business Review. http:// blogs.hbr.org/2011/02/ demystifying-mentoring/. Accessed January 1, 2014.

19. Self Authorship and Transitions Development. http:// studentdevelopmenttheory.wordpress .com/self-authorship-and- transitions/. Accessed January 1, 2014.

Made in the USA
Las Vegas, NV
21 May 2024

90216074R00105